FIRST AID
for
HORSES

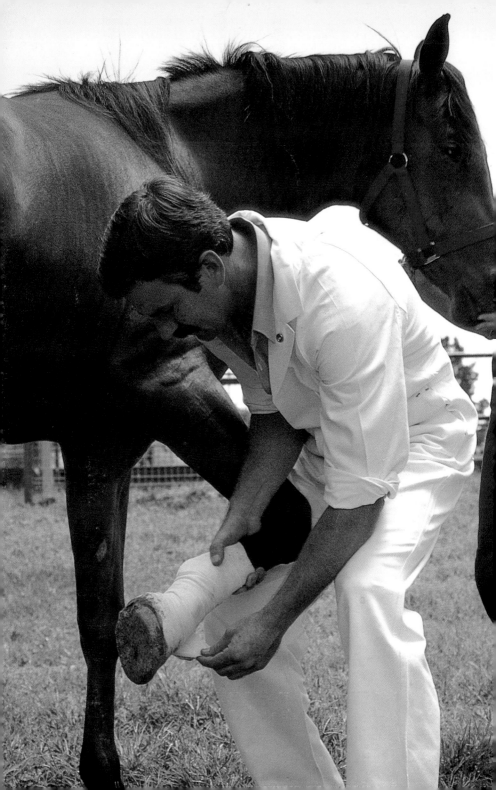

FIRST AID

for

HORSES

The essential quick-reference guide

TIM HAWCROFT
BVSc (Hons), MACVSc, MRCVS

HOWELL BOOK HOUSE

NEW YORK

First U.S. edition 1997

Howell Book House
A Simon & Schuster Macmillan Company
1633 Broadway
New York, NY 10019

MACMILLAN is a registered trademark of Macmillan, Inc.

Library of Congress Cataloging-in-Publication Data

Hawcroft, Tim, 1946–
First aid for horses: the essential quick-reference guide/Tim Hawcroft
p. cm
Originally published: Sydney, N.S.W.: Lansdowne Publishing, 1996
Includes index.
ISBN 0–87605–699–0
1. Horses—Wounds and injuries—Treatment—Handbooks, manuals, etc.
2. Horses—Diseases—Treatment—Handbooks, manuals etc.
3. First aid for animals—Handbooks, manuals, etc. I. Title.
SF951.H3225 1997   96–7232 CIP
636.1'08960252—dc20

Printed in Singapore

10 9 8 7 6 5 4 3 2 1

CONTENTS

INTRODUCTION

The ability to react suddenly and to run quickly has always been the horse's greatest source of protection from predators or danger. When a horse senses danger or is frightened, the horse will often react in a wild, violent, blind panic, having no regard for ropes, fences or any other objects. Consequently, horses often suffer a variety of self-inflicted wounds.

Some injuries and illnesses are caused by man, however. Stressful exercise, especially galloping, can be responsible for severe injury to the limbs. The horse is also subject to injury or disease through incorrect handling, stabling and shoeing. Reckless riding over uneven ground may cause a fracture, a haphazard worming programme may contribute to colic, and careless tethering of a horse to a barbed-wire fence may result in severe lacerations and bleeding if the horse becomes frightened.

Usually an injury or sickness requires some form of First Aid. You never know when you may be confronted with a situation where a horse needs treatment for a life-threatening, serious or simple type of injury or sickness. Perhaps you have come face to face with such a situation and could not help because you didn't know how.

This book of practical First Aid is designed for owners and horse lovers, in fact for all caring persons who want to learn about, update, or extend their knowledge of First Aid for the horse. The information in this book, combined with experience, will give the reader the confidence and the skill to administer First Aid to a horse whenever required.

To save a horse's life, to prevent an injury or sickness worsening, to help a horse recover or to give a distressed horse some comfort and compassion are rewarding experiences for those who render First Aid.

THE CONCEPT OF FIRST AID

When a horse is injured or sick, many people do not know how to help. It may be because they do not not know how to approach and handle a horse, they fear the horse's reaction to their approach or they do not know how to administer First Aid.

First Aid is not a new concept. Horse owners and others have been practising it for generations. First Aid information has been passed around by word of mouth but in recent times the media, authors, veterinarians and pony clubs have been disseminating it. The most practical understanding of the term First Aid is in its literal interpretation: it is the *First* Aid, help or treatment that is given to an injured or sick horse.

Minor, uncomplicated problems, such as a bee sting, grass seed penetration, simple cuts and abrasions, may only need a first treatment, or at the most, repetitions of it. The treatment starts and finishes on site or at the stable. Serious and life-threatening injuries and illness, such as fractures, arterial bleeding and poisoning, need not only First Aid on site or at the stable but require further treatment by a veterinarian.

When an injury or illness occurs at or away from the stable, such as on a roadway in the case of a car accident, there is usually no veterinarian present. Whatever First Aid is given depends on the knowledge, skill, initiative and confidence of the owner or onlooker and the nature of the horse's injury or illness. First Aid may range from something very simple such as comforting the horse, to assessing the horse's condition, perhaps moving the horse to safety and then giving the treatment thought necessary at the time.

Remember that *First* Aid is the first treatment and whatever treatment you can give is better than none at all.

HOW TO USE THIS BOOK

Familiarise yourself with the book's design, the location of various sections and their content. In doing so, you will be able to refer to the book for information in a calm, confident and speedy manner, especially in emergency situations. For ease of reference, we have set out the techniques, injuries and illnesses in alphabetical order. A detailed index in the back of the book will quickly guide you to any information you need.

If you are in a situation where a horse requires First Aid and you are unsure of the action you should take, we suggest you refer to the following sections in this order:

1. First Aid Priorities (see page 11)
2. The Injured or Ill Horse (see page 18)
3. When to Call Your Veterinarian (see page 28)
4. First Aid for Injuries and Illness (see page 52)

These sections offer practical guidance and back-up information so that you can determine what procedure to adopt to treat a particular injury or illness.

Although this book will serve you well in an emergency situation, it is best to be prepared. The purpose of the First Aid Kit section is to prompt you to set up a First Aid kit of your own. Likewise the section on Accident and Illness Prevention is there to remind you of the old adage: prevention is better than cure.

To achieve competence in any activity involving skill you must practise. The sections dealing with The Injured or Ill Horse and Techniques You Should Know contain procedures you should learn. The more you practise and the closer that practice is to reality, the more proficient and confident you will be when facing a real life situation.

IMPORTANT
Always keep your veterinarian's telephone number handy.

FIRST AID KIT

• Store the First Aid kit in a suitable container, readily accessible, portable, and marked for easy identification.

• Clean any soiled instruments after use and if necessary restock the kit.

• Every six months check to see that all is in working order, for example test the torch (flashlight) batteries.

• The kit should contain the following items:

– Antibiotic powder

– Antibiotic pressure pack spray

– Bucket (clean)

– Eye dropper

– Gauze swabs

– Hydrogen peroxide 3%

– Mercurochrome (antiseptic solution)

– Paraffin oil

– Rectal thermometer (same as for human use)

– Roll of adhesive bandage (7.5cm (3in) wide)

– Roll of cotton crepe bandage (7.5cm (3in) wide)

– Roll of cotton gauze (5cm (2in) wide)

– Roll of cottonwool (absorbent cotton)

– Scissors (sharp, pointed, 10cm (4in) long)

– Syringe (plastic, 20ml)

– Tinture of iodine (anti-bacterial, anti-fungal solution)

– Torch (flashlight)

– Tweezers (forceps)

– Vetwrap bandage (10cm (4in) wide)

FIRST AID PRIORITIES

• Keep calm and work methodically.
• In any severe or critical injury or illness, treat shock by keeping the horse calm and warm (see page 84).

1. Life-threatening injuries or illness
• First treat life-threatening conditions. Such signs as:
– Severe bleeding (blood pulsating or flowing freely from a wound) (see page 34).
– No sign of breathing (see page 48).
– No heartbeat (pulse) (see page 34 and 49).
• Call the veterinarian.
• The procedures for resuscitation and restoring heartbeat are recommended for newborn and young foals only and are not applicable to the horse because of its size and mass.

2. Non-life threatening injuries or illness accompanied by severe pain
• Next treat injuries or illness which are causing severe pain but are not life threatening, such as a fracture or extensive burn.
• Approach the horse with caution.
• Your treatment should be concerned with preventing the injury from worsening.
• Call the veterinarian.

3. Minor injuries or illness
• Minor injuries such as a slight abrasion or cut come last in order of priorities for treatment.
• Treat at the stable if you know how.
• Call the veterinarian if the injury becomes inflamed and/or the horse develops a temperature.

ACCIDENT AND ILLNESS PREVENTION

RIDING

• Allow the horse to pick the way in rough country or on steep inclines.
• Travel at a speed where you are in control.
• Avoid galloping past other horses.
• Avoid riding on main roads.
• Do not ride at night on a road that carries traffic.
• Obey traffic laws when riding on a roadway.
These may be:
– Ride or drive as close as possible to the appropriate side of the roadway.
– Do not ride on footpaths, sidewalks or pavements.
– Use recognised traffic signals and obey traffic lights when moving away from the kerb, changing direction or stopping.
– Travel in single file if riding in a group.
• Motorists must give way to an agitated horse if the rider requests or signals the motorist to do so, but to ensure safety be certain the motorist is aware of your intentions.

STABLE

• A doorway of 2.4m (8ft) minimum height and 1.3m (4½ft) wide allows the horse to pass through without brushing the doorway.
– The door should open outward to a full 180° and secured so that it does not close on the handler or horse as they are walking through.
– Both the top and bottom halves of the door should be firmly secured with bolts on the outside.
– The doors and the stable walls should be solid to prevent the horse injuring itself when kicking.

Do you know?
• Most accidents occur because simple safety precautions are unknown, ignored or practised carelessly.
• Some accidents can't be helped; for example, a horse in a blind panic, frightened by a thunder-storm, runs into a fence.

• The window opening should be large enough to allow the horse's head to pass through.
• The electric light and power system should be out of the horse's reach.
• The feed tin (manger) is best located in a corner of the stable, attached to the wall at a suitable height. The feed tin should be made of heavy plastic or tin with rounded edges.
• Never smoke, light a match or carry a naked light into the stable. There is the ever-present danger of the straw bedding catching fire.

YARD AND PADDOCK

• The yard and paddock should be kept clean and securely fenced to about 1.8m (6ft) high. The fence should be made of material that is not dangerous to the horse on contact; for example, solid wooden posts and rails.
• Avoid the presence of barbed-wire, jagged tin, protruding nails and the like.

TRANSPORTING

• A strong, well-fitting head stall (headcollar) and lead to secure the horse in the float is essential.
• The horse may be a victim of travel stress leading to dehydration, colic, diarrhea or pneumonia. To prevent this happening, undertake pre-travel preparation, giving attention to the horse's feet, diet, worming, exercise and general health.
• Feed the horse two hours before the journey.
• Provide a hay net for nutrition and to alleviate the boredom of the journey.
• Curtail grain in the diet 48 hours before the journey.
• Fit the horse with leg and tail bandages, knee boots, hock boots and rug. The rug should be a heavy duty one if the weather is cold and a fly sheet if it is hot, as horses tend to sweat more freely when nervous and confined.

Right: Fencing should be safe and strong. This fence is suitable for all types of horses.

Right: Barbed-wire should not be used on a fence to contain horses.

Left: A gently sloping ramp is important for loading horses.

Left: A horse should be tied securely, using a quick-release knot, to a sturdy object such as a post at about wither height. Alternatively, it is also recommended that you tie your horse to something breakable, such as a loop of string attached to a secure post or rail. The reason for this is that if disaster strikes, the horse will pull away, break the string and free itself with minimum or no injury.

LOADING THE HORSE ONTO THE TRAILER

• The ramp should be nearly level with the ground surface when loading the horse. It should be covered with non-slip matting to deaden the clatter of the horse's hooves, so that the horse does not take fright.

• Some horses scramble or rush up the ramp, with the risk of the handler being trampled or crushed against the side of the trailer or float.

• Tempt a nervous horse to walk onto the float with a handful of oats; have them wear a blindfold or follow another horse.

• Encourage a horse by a tap on the rump with a long-handled whip or by pulling the horse in with a long rope looped around the rump.

• Always put a nervous horse that travels badly last on a multi-horse float. If trouble develops while in transit, the horse is within easy reach and can be removed quickly if necessary.

• Tie the horse securely with a quick-release knot. Allow sufficient rope for head movement, but not so much that the horse becomes tangled in it.

• A well-padded partition between each horse reduces the danger of injury. When a very nervous horse is on a float with other horses, leave the partitions next to that horse empty to minimise injury and feelings of claustrophobia.

• A hay net or nosebag is useful on long journeys to provide nutrition and to act as a source of comfort.

• If the journey is lengthy, at some stage the horses will have to be removed from the float to be watered and to alleviate any stiffness or swelling of the legs.

• When unloading, first untie the horse before lowering the tailgate or ramp.

• Check the trailer frequently for roadworthiness paying particular attention to tyres, lights and tailgate fastenings. Drive with caution; avoid sudden stopping or change of direction.

Do you know?

A reluctant horse can be encouraged to load by taking two lunge lines or ropes and attaching one end of each to string loops on either side of the trailer. Two helpers are needed to walk past each other, crossing the lines behind the horse, keeping them well above the hocks. As the lines close in, the horse should move forwards.

TYING UP

- Always tie the horse to a sturdy object at wither height, such as a post, with a rope lead of suitable length and strength.
- If the rope is too long, the horse is likely to become tangled in it.
- Do not use reins to tie up the horse.
- Tie the horse out of kicking and biting range of other horses.
- Use a quick-release knot which is secure and releases immediately the tail is pulled.

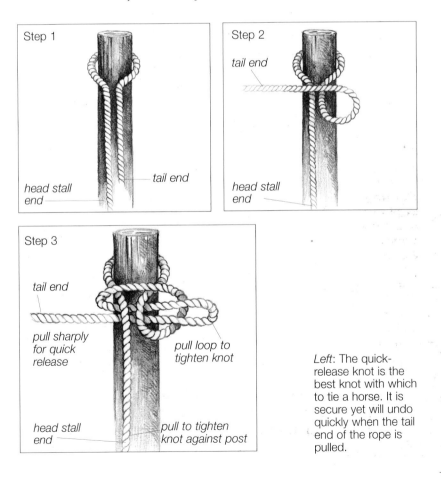

Step 1

tail end

head stall end

Step 2

tail end

head stall end

Step 3

tail end

pull sharply for quick release

pull loop to tighten knot

head stall end

pull to tighten knot against post

Left: The quick-release knot is the best knot with which to tie a horse. It is secure yet will undo quickly when the tail end of the rope is pulled.

17

THE INJURED OR
ILL HORSE

Approaching, Catching, Leading, Restraining and Assessing

A seriously injured or ill horse is usually easy to approach and catch as the horse is often in some degree of shock. A horse with a minor injury or illness may be more difficult to approach because the horse is nervous and perhaps frightened that your approach may aggravate the pain. An injured horse may strike out when you touch a painful area.

APPROACHING, CATCHING AND LEADING

• Do not approach the horse directly from the front or from the rear. Approach the horse from the left-hand (near) side because the horse's normal training has been to accept approach from this side.
• As you approach slowly, speak to the horse quietly but confidently and hold out your hand to rub the horse's neck gently. Quietly and calmly slip the lead around the neck and when you think the horse is ready, put on the head stall and clip the lead to it. If the horse appears nervous as you approach, stop until the horse calms down, then continue.
• With a horse that is difficult to catch, try a reward, for example, bread, keeping any gear such as the head stall and lead out of sight.
• To lead the horse, walk on the left (near) side, halfway between the head and shoulder. Excess lead is looped in the left hand while the right hand holds the lead about 30cm (1ft) from the head ensuring a strong grip should the horse attempt to break away.

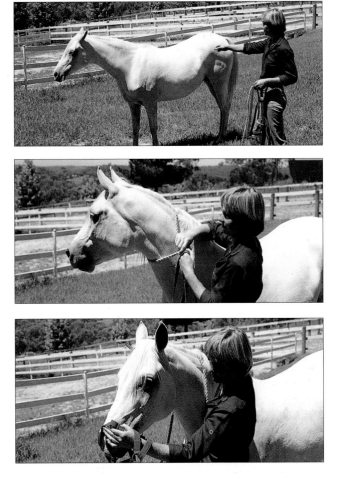

Left: Always take a head stall with lead attached and approach the horse from the left side.

Left: Slip the lead around the horse's neck.

Left: Secure the head stall on the horse's head.

Left: Walk on the left side, between the horse's head and shoulder.

19

RESTRAINING

• Restraint is holding a horse in a controlled manner under various conditions.

• The degree and type of restraint vary with the horse's level of education, maturity, temperament and type of injury or disease. For example, all horses when being examined or treated should wear a head stall (headcollar) and lead, held by an assistant standing on the same side as the person giving First Aid. For a quiet horse with a simple injury such as a cut or abrasion this should be sufficient. If a horse is nervous or in pain, a twitch should be applied. However, if the horse is head shy then gripping the loose skin at the side of the neck may be the best form of restraint.

• Always begin with minimal restraint and if the horse does not respond, progress from there.

• Some horses require sedation by a veterinarian to achieve your purpose.

Using head stall (headcollar) and Lead

• If you control a horse's head, you basically control the rest of the body and limbs. If you have no control over the horse's head, dealing with the horse is almost impossible.

• An assistant, preferably an experienced person, should hold the horse's head and stand on the same side as the person giving First Aid. If the horse is frightened or hurt during the procedure, the horse will tend to jump away from both the person giving First Aid and the assistant.

• The assistant can pull the horse's head towards himself or herself, causing the hindquarters to swing away from the person giving First Aid, who would otherwise be kicked by the hind leg of the horse.

• The assistant can distract the horse by jiggling the lead attached to the head stall (headcollar), by rubbing the horse's head with the free hand and by talking quietly and calmly to the horse.

Gripping the Skin of the Neck

• Gripping the skin of the neck is a very good technique to use on horses that prove difficult when touched around the head. If the horse will not cooperate in being handled and the procedure (such as putting a bandage on the hind leg) takes very little time, a handful of loose skin on the side of the neck towards the base can be gripped and squeezed as tightly as possible. The procedure must be completed quickly because the hand will soon tire and the pressure will weaken to the point where it no longer restrains the horse.

Twisting the Ear

• Starting at the horse's neck, rub your hand upwards to the base of the ear and gently wrap your hand completely around it before applying pressure. Do not make a quick grab at the ear as this will frighten the horse, often causing the horse to half rear and jump away. You can twist and squeeze the ear with your hand as hard as you like without doing damage. Apply just enough pressure to provide the restraint that enables you to carry out the procedure.
• Take care when you use this restraint technique. If used too much and with excessive pressure, the horse may become head shy.

Do you know?
This form of restraint is banned in the UK.

Applying the Twitch

• There are numerous types of twitches with various positions of attachment to the horse. The oldest type is a wooden handle about a metre (yard) long with a rope loop fixed to the end; large enough to accommodate a horse's muzzle plus the handler's hand.
– The twitch should be applied to the upper lip by an assistant while you perform First Aid. If the horse resists, get another assistant to grip the skin of the horse's neck and ear. If this is unsuccessful, the twitch may be applied to the lower third of the ear. Do not apply the twitch to the lower lip because the lip may be torn if the horse rears suddenly.

Do you know?
A twitch with a handle made of stiff, heavy rubber is safest for the holder and most effective on the horse.

Right: Gripping the neck is a successful technique for restraining horses that are sensitive around the nose and ears.

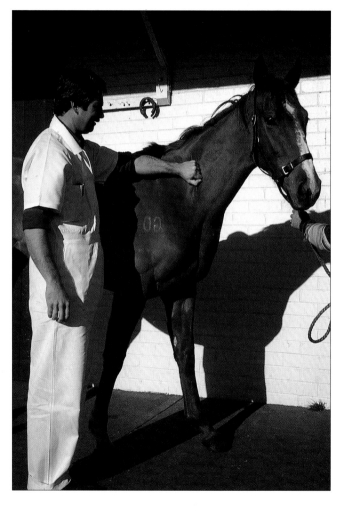

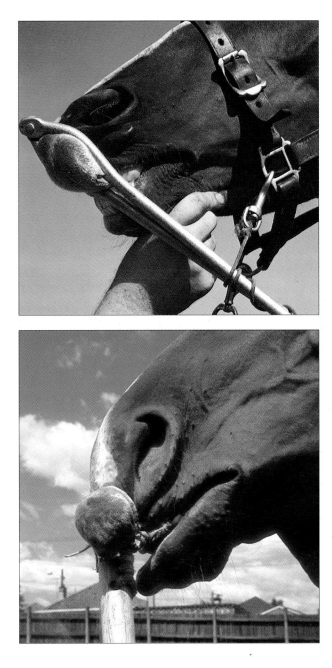

Left: A commercially available metal twitch.

Left: A wooden handled twitch firmly applied to the upper lip for effective restraint.

– When applying the twitch, the assistant should stand to the side of the horse, never in front.

– The rope loop is applied over as much of the upper lip as can be gathered into the loop. The handle of the twitch is twisted to tighten the loop only to the point where there is firm pressure on the lip and so the loop will not slip off. The handle should not be twisted so quickly that the loop snaps tightly onto the nose, causing the horse to rear and strike.

– Immediately the twitch is tightened, attach the lead on the head stall (headcollar) to the handle of the twitch with two half-hitch knots. This precaution is taken in case the horse rears and pulls the twitch from the assistant's hands; the assistant is still holding the lead, preventing the twitch handle from flaying around.

– If the horse resists the twitch, a slight tightening or loosening of it may be effective.The person holding the twitch can help by changing the pressure of the twitch, talking to the horse, rubbing the horse's neck with one hand and generally distracting the horse.

– An attempt by the horse to strike with the foreleg can be anticipated if the horse becomes restless. In this case, the pressure on the twitch should be released. There is no need to have a twitch on tightly for a lengthy period. The assistant can relax the twitch while the person giving First Aid is resting and tighten it when the person resumes.

• Some twitches do not have a handle: these include ring twitches and commercially available clamps. These types of twitches can be applied and secured to the head stall (headcollar), leaving one hand free, and if the horse pulls free there is no flaying handle to hit the assistant. Their disadvantages are that they are slower to apply and release and they can only exert a certain amount of pressure which can be crucial when dealing with a fractious horse.

Holding Up a Front Leg

• Restraining the horse by holding up a front leg is a useful method only with horses that have been well-handled and are familiar with having their feet picked up. Position the horse so that it is standing squarely on all four feet, bearing weight equally, thus making it easier to pick up a foot.

• An assistant standing on the same side of the horse as the person giving First Aid, lifts the foreleg on that side, off the ground. This prevents the horse kicking with the hind leg located on that side. The horse should not be allowed to lean against the assistant as this position would allow the horse to kick with the hind leg located on that side.

Holding a Horse Down

• Use this method when the horse is lying outstretched and is spasmodically struggling to get up but is unable to do so. Rather than letting the horse flounder with the risk of further injury, put a head stall (headcollar) and lead on the horse. Prevent the horse from getting up by kneeling on the extended neck and putting a hand on the head, with your full weight.

Restraining Foals and Weanlings

• When held around the head, young foals tend to rear backwards. They often strike the head, and may thus suffer a fatal concussion or fracture. Young foals may rush backwards, lose balance and fall over or crash into a wall.

• The foal is best handled in close proximity to the mother. Approach the foal slowly, cupping one arm under and around the neck and the other around the rump to form a cradle so that the foal cannot rush forward or backward.

• Weanlings tend to rear and flip over backwards if frightened. Make sure the weanling is backed up against a wall or fence, with someone firmly holding the tail near the base, to prevent the weanling from sitting down.

Right: A horse is prevented from standing if the extended neck is knelt on.

Below: This weanling is well held up against a fence. The tail is being supported to prevent the horse sitting down and flipping over backwards.

• The person at the head restrains the weanling by rubbing a hand on the neck and working gradually up to the ear, cupping a hand around the ear and squeezing hard. If further restraint is required, the other ear is gripped in the same manner.

Look at the colour of the gums
• If pale or white and there is no sign of severe external bleeding, the horse could be suffering from shock or internal blood loss. Call your veterinarian.
• If the gums are pink, that is a good sign that there is no major blood loss externally or internally.

Check the horse's breathing
• First examine the horse's respiration from a distance of about 2m (6ft). Rapid, irregular, noisy, shallow or painful respiration is abnormal and requires veterinary attention.
• The breathing rate can be detected by gently placing the hand over one nostril and feeling the air movement, or by observation of rib or nostril movement. Normal respiration rate is 8 to 14 breaths per minute.

Carefully run your hand over the horse's body
• Look and feel for a wound, swelling or pain.
• Check the movement of the limbs and note if there is pain, swelling, a grating sensation, a floppy limb irregular in appearance, or whether the horse cannot move one or more limbs. These signs indicate the limb may be broken (fractured) or joint dislocated.

If the horse seems sound encourage walking
• If the horse flops down, walks on three legs and carries the fourth, limps, staggers, refuses to move, or breathes in a painful panting fashion, rug to maintain warmth and counteract shock. Call your veterinarian.

ASSESSING THE HORSE'S CONDITION

27

WHEN TO CALL YOUR VETERINARIAN

The following information may serve as a guide if you are uncertain when to call your veterinarian.

- **Birth difficulty** If no foal appears after about 25 minutes of obvious contractions and straining; or the mare gives up after straining for 20 minutes; or part of the foal appears, for example the leg, but nothing else appears after 20 minutes of straining.
- **Bleeding heavily** From any part of the body; will not stop. Apply pressure to stop the bleeding (see page 34).
- **Blood in urine** Obvious blood in urine.
- **Breathing difficulty** Gasping, noisy breathing; blue tongue.
- **Burns** Fairly extensive; or if in doubt see page 68.
- **Choke (Choking)** Appears distressed; extends head and neck; salivates; coughs; grunts; strikes ground; food and saliva may be regurgitated through nostrils.
- **Collapse or loss of balance** Over-reaction to external stimuli; depression; staggering; knuckling over; walking in circles; down, unable to get up; general muscle tremor; rigidity; paddling movements of legs; coma.
- **Diarrhea** Putrid, fluid diarrhea with or without blood or abdominal pain.
- **Injury** Severe continuous pain; severe lameness; cut with bone exposed; puncture wound especially on the chest or abdomen.
- **Itching** Continual, uncontrollable biting and tearing at the skin; skin broken and bleeding.
- **Pain** Severe, continuous or spasmodic eg. colic.

• **Poisoning** Chemical, snake or plant. Try to retain sample for veterinarian to identify type of poisoning.
• **Straining continuously** Attempting to defecate (pass a motion) or urinate with little or no result.

• **Abortion (miscarriage)** Expulsion of the foetus.
• **Afterbirth retained** If retained for eight hours.
• **Appetite loss** Not eating; depressed in conjunction with other signs, such as painful breathing, diarrhea, lying down, pain, sweating.
• **Breathing difficulty** Laboured breathing (heaving); rapid and shallow breathing with or without cough.
• **Diarrhea** Motion fluid.
• **Eye problems** Tears streaming down cheeks; eyelids partially or completely closed; cornea (surface of eye) hazy, opaque or bluish-white in colour.
• **Foreign body swallowed** Better for veterinarian to assess early, rather than wait until a possible life-threatening situation develops.
• **Frostbite and/or hypothermia** Low body temperature usually associated with sub-zero temperatures (see pages 77 and 80).
• **Injuries** Not urgent but liable to become infected; a cut through full thickness of skin needing stitching; puncture wound of foot; sudden acute lameness.
• **Itching** Self-mutilating; irritated or damaged skin; bleeding sores.
• **Swelling** Hot, hard and painful or discharging.

• **Appetite loss** Not eating; no other symptom.
• **Diarrhea** Cow-like; no indication of abdominal pain; no sign of blood; no straining.
• **Itching** Moderate; no damage by self-mutilation.
• **Lameness** Ability to bear weight on leg; not affecting eating or other functions.
• **Thirst** Excessive drinking, often paired with excessive urination.

CALL SAME DAY

WAIT 24 HOURS BEFORE CALLING

TECHNIQUES YOU SHOULD KNOW

Bandaging

In serious, life-threatening situations such as severe bleeding, apply a pad and firm bandage first to staunch the flow, and delay cleaning the wound until later.

Steps in bandaging

• If possible, clean the wound of any debris and clip any invasive hair surrounding the wound, then cover the wound with a cotton gauze pad or a clean handkerchief.

• Wrap a cotton gauze bandage firmly over the gauze pad covering the wound.

• Secure the gauze bandage by firmly wrapping an adhesive bandage over it, allowing some of the adhesive bandage to stick to the hair on either side of the gauze bandage.

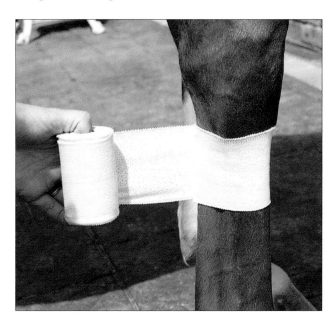

Left: The correct way to apply an adhesive bandage.

Types of Bandage

Adhesive

• Provides a non-slip covering difficult for the horse to remove.
• Should never be applied directly to a wound except in an emergency.
• Ideal size is 7.5cm (3in) wide.
• To avoid applying it too tightly, unroll a manageable portion first before wrapping it on.

Cotton gauze

• Gauze bandages alone tend to slip and are easily torn off by the horse.
• A gauze bandage is usually covered with an adhesive bandage to make it secure, especially if the adhesive is applied so that it sticks to the hair as well as to the gauze bandage.
• The best type is one that adheres to itself. This type does not unravel and tends to conform to the shape of the horse, making it firmer and not so bulky.
• The end of the bandage can be secured with adhesive bandage. Another way is to cut the end down the middle to about 25cm (10in). Tie a knot at the base of the two tape-like pieces to prevent further tearing and tie the tapes to secure the bandage.
• The ideal size is 5cm (2in) wide.

Vetwrap bandage

• A strong, self-adhering bandage which will not unravel or slip and can be used more than once.
• Vetwrap is soft and conforms to that part of the horse being bandaged.
• It is used to cover a gauze bandage or dressing.
• Vetwrap is not as tough as an adhesive bandage and is more easily torn and pulled off by the horse.
• One size only is commercially available, namely 10cm (4in) wide.

Keep in mind

• Bandages should never be too tight nor too loose.
• If blood from a wound is coming through a bandage, do not remove the bandage but apply a slightly tighter adhesive bandage over it.
• If a very firm to tight bandage is on a limb for any length of time, for example 30 minutes, check the limb below the bandage. If the limb is swollen, cold to touch or does not react to pain when pinched, remove the bandage immediately and, if necessary, apply a new bandage less tightly.

Leg

• Apply gauze pad to the wound after cleaning and cutting away any invasive hair.
• Wind cotton gauze bandage around the leg three or four times and secure with a similar adhesive bandage partly adhering to the horse's hair.
• When applying the cotton gauze bandage near a joint, make a figure eight above and below the joint.
• Before applying a bandage around the knee joint, first feel for the bone under the skin at the back of the knee towards the outside. Do not cover this bone with bandage as a nasty pressure sore may develop.
• Always stand to the side of the leg, facing the hindquarters, when applying or removing a bandage; stoop over or bend at the knees, but never kneel.
• The beginning and end of all bandaging should be secure; bandages that slip can become dangerous.
• Apply the bandage with a firm, even pressure and check to see that leg does not swell. If there is swelling remove the bandage and start again.
• Cottonwool (absorbent cotton) under the bandages can sometimes form hard balls that act as pressure points, so use layers of sponge rubber under the bandage to ensure an even distribution of pressure.

HOW TO BANDAGE

Bleeding — How to Stop

• Remain calm.
• Immobilise the horse with a head stall (headcollar) and lead or if this is unsuccessful use another method of restraint (see page 20).
• Apply pressure directly to the site with a clean wad of cloth in the hand, or if no cloth available, with the hand or fingers only.
• Apply an icepack to the site if the source of bleeding is inaccessible.
• See page 64 for further information on controlling bleeding.
• *Do not* dab or wipe the site as this tends to promote bleeding.
• *Do not* clean the site until bleeding has stopped as this might encourage fresh bleeding.

Heartbeat and Pulse — How to Check

• The normal pulse of the horse varies according to breed, age and weight.
• The normal pulse rate ranges from 30 to 42 beats per minute.
• The pulse is a reflection of the heartbeat; it is an indicator of blood circulation.

Where to Feel the Pulse

• To obtain a correct reading, the horse must be calm and quiet.
• Place a finger (not the thumb) on an artery that is close to the surface of the skin.
• An artery that is easy to locate is the one that passes under the lower jaw.

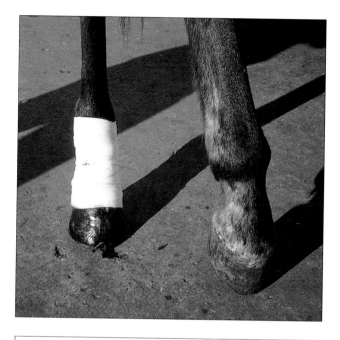

Left: Bleeding controlled by firmly applied bandage.

Left: Feeling for pulse in the artery which runs under the lower jaw.

Where to Feel the Heartbeat

• The heartbeat is best located behind the left elbow. Place the palm of the hand on the chest behind the point of the left elbow. The heartbeat is easier to detect if the left (near) foreleg is positioned about 30cm (1ft) in advance of the right (off) foreleg.
If the heartbeat is outside the average resting heartbeat (30 to 42 beats per minute), call your veterinarian.

Leg Fracture

The following methods of treating a leg fracture are temporary pending the arrival of your veterinarian.

Robert Jones Bandage Technique

The Robert Jones Bandage Technique described below gives good immobilisation and support and does not interfere with circulation:
• Evenly wrap several layers of cottonwool (absorbent cotton) around the fractured limb well above and below as well as over the fracture site.

1. The Robert Jones Bandage Technique begins with wrapping layers of cottonwool (absorbent cotton) around the fractured limb.

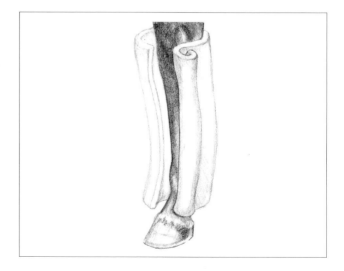

• Compress the layers of cottonwool (absorbent cotton) by firmly wrapping several rolls of gauze bandage over them.

• Finally, wrap a number of layers of adhesive bandage over the gauze bandage and nearby hair.

• Check to see that circulation has not been interfered with (see page 33).

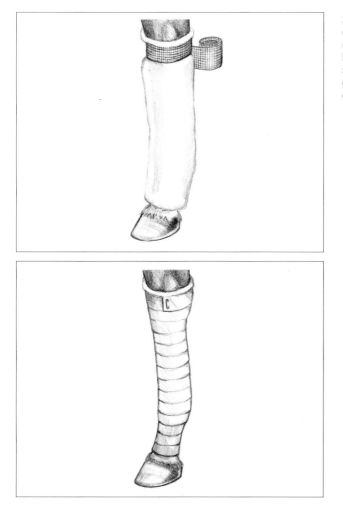

2. Compress the cottonwool (absorbent cotton) by firmly wrapping several layers of gauze bandage over them.

3. Finally, wrap a number of layers of adhesive bandage around the gauze bandage and nearby hair.

Splint

A splint can be readily improvised by:
• Wrapping a pillow or roll of cottonwool (absorbent cotton) around the leg, with the fracture in the centre of the wrapping.
• Bind the wrapping to the leg with gauze bandage, applying it as tightly as possible.
• Incorporate a broom handle in the bandaging to add extra rigidity.
• Finally, tightly apply a few layers of 7.5cm (3in) adhesive bandage.

Medicine — How to Administer

Medicines come in many forms: pellet, powder, liquid, paste, tablet, capsule, bolus (a large tablet), ointment, drops or injection. How the medicine is to be given, for example by mouth or stomach tube, and in what form depends on such factors as its type and palatability, the condition and temperament of the horse, and the owner's temperament.
By nature, horses are suspicious of any unpalatable materials in their food and will sort it out or reject their food completely.

Pelleted Preparations in Feed

• Numerous vitamin and mineral supplements and worm preparations are pelleted to prevent wastage. They contain additives such as flavouring to make them palatable so they can be mixed in as part of the normal feed.

Powders and Liquids in Feed

• Provided they are palatable, powders and liquids can be thoroughly mixed with the feed to prevent the horse selectively avoiding the powder or liquid and eating the remainder of the feed. Unfortunately, powders tend to collect in the bottom of the feed tin

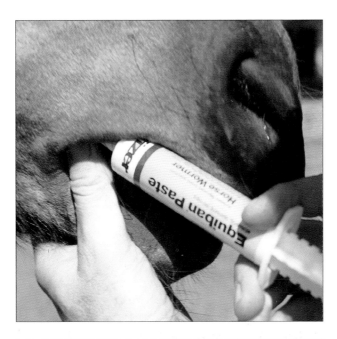

Left: When administering paste by syringe ensure the horse swallows the dose by holding its head up after injecting the medicine.

Left: Administer tablets by hand with the horse's mouth held open by a gag to avoid being bitten.

39

(manger) in inaccessible corners, and some of the powder is blown out of the feed tin when the horse blows through the nostrils while eating. If powder and liquid preparations are not palatable, mix them with molasses or honey and then mix that with the feed, or use a large wooden spoon to wipe the sweet mixture over the horse's tongue.

Powders and Liquids in Drinking Water

• Many electrolyte mixtures in powdered form can be given in the drinking water. Leave the horse in the yard or stable for a number of hours without water. Add the powder or liquid to a bucket about a quarter full of water and offer the water to the horse. When the horse has finished drinking, top up the bucket with fresh water.

Liquids and Pastes by Syringe

• Many worming pastes are now packaged in a syringe. Put a head stall (headcollar) on the horse with a lead attached, then make sure the horse's mouth is empty before introducing the syringe.

• Stand on the left (near) side of the horse's head, facing the horse, and put the syringe in the corner of the mouth so that the nozzle rests on the back of the tongue. After depressing the plunger, ensure that the full dose is swallowed by holding up the horse's head, but not so high that the horse will have difficulty in swallowing.

• If the syringe contains a liquid, don't squirt it rapidly onto the back of the tongue, as some may go into the windpipe and cause inhalation pneumonia. Gently dribble it onto the tongue, allowing sufficient time for the horse to swallow.

40

Tablets, Capsules and Boluses Placed in Mouth

• These forms of medication can be given to the horse by hand. A gag can be used which keeps the horse's mouth open so that you can administer medicine without being bitten.

• To administer medication by hand without a gag, stand facing the horse's head, slightly to the left (near) side. Putting your left hand into the right side of the horse's mouth, grasp a good handful of the tongue and pull it out between the lips on the right side of the mouth. As well as keeping the mouth open, this will prevent the horse from biting you.

• With your right hand, place the tablet, capsule or bolus as far back on the tongue as possible and quickly release the tongue from your left hand. This action carries the tablet into the back of the throat.

• Lubricating the tablet before introducing it and holding the horse's head in a slightly elevated position helps the tablet slide down more smoothly.

• Do not put irritant materials in gelatine capsules as sometimes they become caught in the throat or oesophagus (food pipe), dissolve and release the irritant material with the risk of causing injury.

Drenching with Bottle in Mouth

• To carry out this procedure, elevate the horse's head sufficiently to allow the liquid to flow to the back of the throat. If the head cannot be held high enough by hand, attach a rope to the noseband of the head stall (headcollar) and raise the head by pulling on a rope thrown over a rafter. Introduce a plastic bottle with a long neck into the mouth in a gap between the teeth.

• Slowly trickle the solution into the horse's mouth, allowing plenty of time to swallow. There is the danger of fluid getting into the windpipe, causing secondary pneumonia, so drench slowly.

Right: Medicating a horse by stomach tube through nasal passage is a safe procedure when performed by trained personnel.

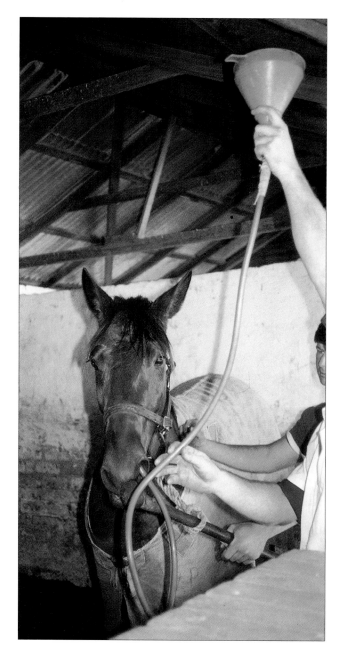

Left: Intra-muscular injection is a quick, efficient procedure used by veterinarians to administer medicine.

Nasal Administration of Drugs

• The stomach tube is an efficient, safe, professional method of giving liquid medication, but this technique should be left to the veterinary surgeon or trained personnel. In inexperienced hands, the stomach tube may be inadvertently passed into the lungs, resulting in the death of the horse from inhalation pneumonia.

Injections

• This procedure is often used by veterinary surgeons as it is quick, efficient and convenient. Injections can be given under the skin (subcutaneous), into muscle (intra-muscular), into a vein (intravenous) or into a joint space (intra-articular). The type of drug used and the disease being treated determine how and where the injection will be given. This technique should be employed only by veterinary surgeons or trained personnel.

Administration of Drugs via Rectum

• Extreme care should be taken when giving an enema to a foal. Use a soft tube and make sure it is well lubricated with petroleum jelly.

43

• Do not insert the tube more than 10cm (4in) into the rectum, and insert it gently. Allow the fluid to flow by gravity, which is safer than forcing it in under pressure and risking rupturing the rectal wall.

Administering Bran Mash

• Sick horses are prone to constipation. Bran mash can be used to encourage a sick or convalescent horse to eat, as well as being an effective means of treating and preventing constipation.
• To make bran mash: place 1kg (2lb) of bran, 30gm (1oz) of salt and 300ml (10fl oz) of molasses into a clean bucket; add 2 litres (30fl oz) of hot water and stir thoroughly. Let the mixture stand for 10 minutes before feeding to the horse.

Administering Ear Drops

• Get an assistant to hold the horse's head firmly while you administer the drops.
• Squeeze four to six drops into the ear canal and gently massage below the ear to work the drops down the ear canal.
• If the horse fidgets just squirt the drops into the ear canal. Stop when the medicine wells up out of the ear canal.

Administering Eye Drops

• Get an assistant to hold the horse's head and tilt it slightly while you administer the medication.
• Gently hold the eyelids apart with your thumb and index finger.
• Administer two drops onto the eyeball. Keep the head tilted for about 20 seconds or the eye drops will roll out and be wasted.

Administering Eye Ointment

• Get an assistant to hold the horse's head while you administer the medication.
• With your thumb, either pull the lower lid down or the upper lid up and lay a strip of eye ointment inside the lid along its full length.
• Close the eyelid. The ointment will melt forming a film over the eyeball and conjunctiva.

Orphan Foal — How to Feed

Some foals have to be hand-fed because the mother died at birth or has no milk or rejects the foal. Or the foal itself, because of weakness or some other reason, is unable to suckle. Colostrum is the name given to the first milk that the mare produces. It is very thick, bright yellow to orange in colour and gives the foal immunity against infection in its early days of life. Colostrum is only produced by the mare for about the first 24 hours after the foal is born and the foal can only absorb the antibodies from it for about the first 36 hours of life. Colostrum is high in vitamins and food value and guards against constipation.

Bottle Feeding

• The foal should be fed every three hours for the first week of life, day and night. Substitute milk can be made up according to this formula: 300ml (10fl oz) cow's milk, 300ml (10fl oz) warm, boiled water, 5ml (1 teaspoon) lime water and 5ml (1 teaspoon) sugar. An alternative formula is 300ml (10fl oz) evaporated or powdered milk, 300ml (10fl oz) water and 5ml (1 teaspoon) sugar. Thereafter the frequency of the feeds should be decreased and the amount given increased. A four-week-old foal is fed four times a day. At each three-hourly feed, the foal should receive 600ml (20fl oz) milk substitute, which can be varied according to individual demand.
• Foals have the ability to suck naturally. If the foal rejects the bottle teat, place your index finger in the foal's mouth. If the foal still does not suck, move the index finger against the roof of the mouth and tongue. Slowly replace the index finger with the teat once sucking has begun.
• The disadvantage of bottle feeding is that it is time-consuming and the labour may be costly.

Right: A foster mother is the best solution for an orphaned foal.

Foster Mother

• The best solution for an orphan foal is to use a foster mother. Some mares are good foster mothers while others will not readily accept an orphan foal and may even reject it. Mares that become a little fractious and unwilling in this situation can be calmed by use of a twitch or tranquilliser. It is wise to introduce an orphan foal to the foster mother with some caution so that no harm is done.

Bucket Feeding

• Apart from a foster mare, this is the best form of feeding because it is effective, easier to implement and less time-consuming than any other method. Initially, a little more time and patience are needed to encourage the foal to feed from a bucket.
• Isolate the foal for a number of hours in a warm, safe environment until the foal is hungry and wants attention. Pour the formula into a plastic bucket with

a wide opening so that the foal will not baulk at putting its head into the bucket. The biggest problem in getting the foal to drink from a bucket is persuading the foal to suck with the head down as a foal suckles from the mother with the head up.

• With the foal's head up, get the foal to suck on your index finger. Gradually, with the foal sucking on your finger, direct the foal's head down until the mouth is in the milk bucket. Withdraw your finger. If the foal doesn't continue sucking after the first attempt, go through the procedure again. Exercise patience and persistence with the foal.

• Hang the bucket in a secure position at a height convenient for the foal to drink at will, and ensure the formula is freely available to the foal. This way the foal will not over-drink. Change the milk and clean the bucket thoroughly twice a day.

Dry Feeding

• Once the foal is several days old and drinking readily from the bucket, set up another bucket similar in shape and position containing about two handfuls of a readily digestible, milk-based, pelleted food. Encourage the foal to eat the pellets by placing a few in the mouth and directing the foal's head to the bucket. Once the foal accepts pellets by eating them readily, make them freely available at all times. Gradually substitute a grain-based pellet when the foal is eating about 1kg (2lb) milk-based pellets per day.

• At four weeks of age, the foal can be weaned completely off prepared milk formula and fed dry pellets and good-quality grains as well as a limited quantity of hay.

Stomach tube

• If the foal is very weak and unable to stand, a tube can be passed into the stomach and secured permanently in position. This procedure is best done by the veterinarian. You can then connect a funnel to the tube and pour the necessary nutritional requirements down the tube every three hours. This routine should be continued until the foal is strong enough to stand and suckle.

Medication

• Even if orphan foals have received colostrum, they should be given a course of antibiotics by the veterinary surgeon as soon after birth as possible as this helps prevent infection.

Resuscitation of Newborn and Young Foals

• The average foal's breathing rate is 10 to 15 breaths per minute.
• The average foal's heartbeat (pulse) is 40 to 58 beats per minute.
• Immediate yet calm treatment is essential for successful resuscitation.

If Breathing has Stopped

• Check the foal's mouth or nose for any foreign body or food obstructing the airway.
• Place the foal on the right (off) side and tilt the head back. Keeping the foal's mouth closed, block the right nostril.
• Place a porous cloth, such as a handkerchief, over the foal's nostril before applying mouth to nose (for cosmetic reasons only).
• Place your open mouth over the foal's left nostril and breathe into the nostril at the rate of 10 to 15 breaths per minute.
• If breathing is restored, keep the foal under observation.
• If breathing is not restored, apply mouth to nose resuscitation at the rate of one breath every four seconds, that is, 15 breaths per minute.

• If breathing is not restored after 10 minutes, the gums and tongue are blue, the pupils are dilated and there is no blinking when the surface of the eye is touched, you can presume the foal is dead.

• Lay the foal on the right (off) side.
• Place the heel of your hand on the chest in the area just behind the foal's left elbow.
• The pressure should be forceful enough to cause compression of the chest wall in the local area with subsequent compression of the heart.
• Give ten quick compressions. If the heartbeat (pulse) is restored, keep the foal under observation.
• If the heartbeat (pulse) is not restored, continue to apply cardiac compression in cycles of ten at the rate of five cycles per minute. When the heartbeat (pulse) is restored, keep the foal under observation.
• If the heartbeat (pulse) is not restored after 10 minutes, the gums and tongue are blue, the pupils are dilated and there is no blinking when the surface of the eye is touched, you can presume the foal is dead.

Temperature — How to Check

• The normal temperature for a horse ranges between 37.7°C (99.5°F) and 38.6°C (101.5°F).
• See your veterinarian if your horse's temperature remains outside that range, as the horse probably has an infection or some other illness.

Taking the Temperature

• An ordinary household thermometer may be used to take the horse's temperature.
• Shake the mercury down below 37.7°C (99.5°F) and smear the thermometer with a non-irritant lubricant such as petroleum jelly.

Right: Take the horse's temperature by inserting a thermometer into the horse's anus and holding for one to two minutes before checking.

• Insert the thermometer into the horse's anus to about 5cm (2in) with the bulb resting against the rectal wall.

• Withdraw the thermometer after one to two minutes and check the reading.

Umbilical Cord — How to Sever and Treat

• If the umbilical cord is intact when the foal is born, it is important to allow it to remain so as long as possible in order to effect a complete transfer of blood from the placenta to the foal.

• In most cases the umbilical cord will break naturally about 5 to 7.5cm (2 to 3in) from the foal's navel when the foal struggles to rise, or when the mare gets to her feet. For the small percentage of cases where the cord fails to break naturally use the following procedure:

Severing and Treating the Cord

• To prevent bleeding, apply a ligature by tightly tying thread soaked in disinfectant around the umbilical cord about 8cm (3in) from the foal's body.

• Cut the cord with scissors soaked in disinfectant 2.5cm (1in) from the ligature, on the placental side.

• Swab the cut end with tincture of iodine (anti-bacterial, anti-fungal solution).

• If the end of the umbilical cord is bleeding after it has broken naturally, control the haemorrhage by tying the cord off with disinfected thread.

FIRST AID FOR INJURIES AND ILLNESS

Abscess

• An abscess is a collection of pus, circumscribed in a sac, and enclosed within the tissues of the body.
• Abscesses may be due to a puncture wound or to a foreign body, such as a nail or grass seed, entering the body and setting up an infection, or to bacteria lodging in an organ after a generalised infection, in which case the abscess might appear on the liver or lungs.

Signs

• Pain felt by the horse when touched at the site of the abscess.
• The horse may be lethargic, without an appetite and/or have a temperature.
• The abscess is at first a hard lump which softens as the abscess matures.
• If abscess bursts, there is a bloody, purulent discharge.

Action

• If a puncture wound is obvious, clean with iodine-based scrub or 3% hydrogen peroxide.
• Remove any foreign body that may be embedded in the wound and cut away surrounding hair.
• Bathe the swelling for 10 minutes twice daily with cottonwool (absorbent cotton) soaked in hot water, gently squeezing any discharge, if present, from the puncture hole.
• If the abscess does not burst, the veterinarian will open the abscess, drain out the pus and administer antibiotics and anti-tetanus vaccine.
• If the abscess continues to drain after being opened, it should be irrigated twice daily using a syringe containing 3% hydrogen peroxide.

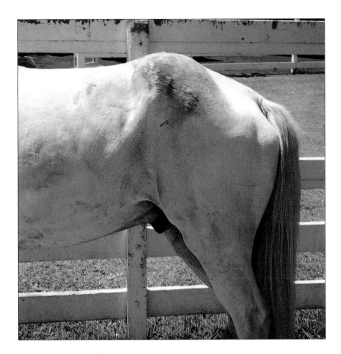

Left: Abscess on the rump — a hard, painful swelling.

Below: This horse is suffering from severe azoturia (tying up).

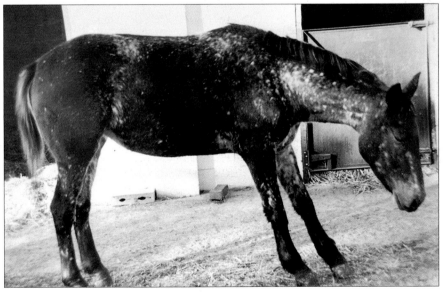

Azoturia (Tying Up)

This condition is sometimes called Monday Morning Disease because sport horses and working horses in good, well-muscled condition exhibit symptoms of tying up on Monday mornings after they had rested and been fed a high-grain diet over the weekend.

Signs

•Characterised by stiffness, pain and muscle tremor involving the muscles of the hindquarters, except in severe cases where the muscles of the forequarters may be involved as well.

Action

• Stop working the horse.
• In all cases except severe ones, walk the horse for 30 minutes. This helps to prevent cramping.
• If the horse is no better, call your veterinarian.
• Keep the horse warm and well rugged.
• Tempt the horse with fluids containing electrolytes (see page 40).
• Eliminate all grains from the horse's diet.
• Offer the horse a bran mash (see page 44) as a mild laxative.

Prevention

• Horses susceptible to frequent tying up should have a low-grain diet.
• Exercise the horse every day, even if it is just walking exercise.
• Vary the level of grain in the diet according to the amount of exercise.

Birth Problems

• The normal presentation is for the foal's front feet to appear with the head resting on the forelegs and one front foot leads the other by about 15cm (6in).
• The mare usually lies down but may stand up during the birth (the labour stage).
• When the head of the foal appears, immediately remove any placental membrane that may be obstructing the foal's nostrils.
• The umbilical cord will break naturally about 5 to 7.5cm (2 to 3in) from the foal's navel when it struggles to rise, or when the mare gets to her feet. (See page 51 for how to treat and sever the umbilical cord.)
• The mare should expel the placental membrane or afterbirth within three hours after foaling.

Do you know?
About 80% of foals are born between 11pm and 1am with the birth (the labour stage) over within 20 minutes or so.

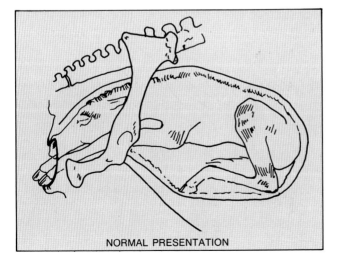

NORMAL PRESENTATION

Left: Normal presentation of the foal.

57

Action

• If you cannot give the First Aid that is required, contact your veterinarian immediately.

• In rendering First Aid at a birth scene, make sure your hands have been scrubbed with a non-irritant antiseptic, for example chlorhexidine, and that you are wearing surgical gloves if available.

Foal present at the vulva

• Scrub your hands and wash around the mare's anus and vulva with a non-irritant antiseptic such as chlorhexidine.

• Make sure your hand and arm is well-lubricated with petroleum jelly.

• If the presentation is normal but the mare cannot expel the foal, take hold of both the foal's forelegs and gently but firmly pull downwards and outwards to assist the passage.

• If only one of the foal's leg is presented, the elbow of the other leg may be caught on the brim of the mare's pelvis. In this case, pull the leg out to bring it almost level with the one that is in a normal position. This action lifts the foal's elbow over the rim of the pelvis thus allowing free passage of the foal.

• Excessive bulging of the mare's anus may indicate the feet of the foal have been pushed towards the mare's rectum by her contractions. If contractions continue, the feet may tear the recto-vaginal wall creating a hole or cavity known as a fistula which may become ulcerated, infected and possibly render the mare infertile. To prevent this, place your hand inside the vagina and guide the foal's feet to the vaginal opening as the mare contracts.

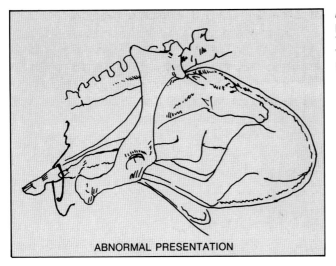

ABNORMAL PRESENTATION

Left: Abnormal presentation — forefeet presented with head not presented.

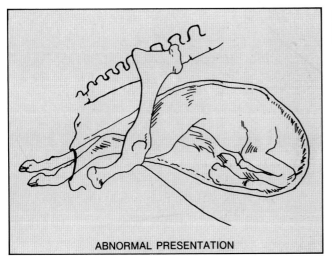

ABNORMAL PRESENTATION

Left: Abnormal presentation — hind feet presented first.

Birth problems needing immediate veterinary attention

• Forefeet presented but head back in uterus resting on foal's flank.
• Foal on its back with soles of forefeet and lower jaw uppermost.
• Foal doubled on itself so that the head, forefeet and hind feet are presented together.
• Hind feet are presented first, soles facing upwards.
• Buttocks and tail of foal are presented (breech presentation).
• Twin foals.

No foal present at vulva

The veterinary surgeon should be called immediately if:
• No foal appears after 25 minutes of obvious straining and contractions.
• There are no obvious contractions and the mare is continually getting up and down, showing signs of pain by kicking, swishing tail and looking at flanks.
• After 15 minutes of obvious contractions and straining, the mare appears to give up and her efforts for the next 30 minutes are weak and less frequent.

Newborn foal not breathing

• Check the airways to see that they are clear.
If necessary, wipe away any placental membranes or mucus that may be blocking the nostrils or mouth.
• Wrap the foal in a warm blanket and lay it down in a position with the head lower than the rest of the body. Warmth is very important, and the head-down position allows the blood to flow more freely to the brain.
• Rub the foal's chest briskly with a towel in an attempt to stimulate breathing.
• If the newborn foal is still not breathing, apply resuscitation (see page 48).

Afterbirth not expelled

The afterbirth may be expelled from the mare before she gets to her feet after foaling. On average, it is expelled within three hours. If the afterbirth is not expelled within eight hours, take the following action:

• Tie the membranes in a knot to prevent them dragging on the ground as there is a risk that the mare may tread on them and tear them with her hind feet.

• If the retained afterbirth is obvious, remove it manually by pulling on it with firm, even tension.

• Stop pulling if the afterbirth does not give way; you could cause haemorrhage, damage to the lining of the uterus and infection due to the membranes tearing and a small portion of the afterbirth remaining in the uterus.

• Call your veterinarian as it may be necessary to administer a drug to aid in separation of afterbirth from the attachments in the uterus.

• Once the afterbirth is removed, it is important to lay out the membranes on the ground to check that all the afterbirth has been expelled.

Bites and Stings

FLY AND MOSQUITO BITES

• Stable flies and mosquitoes can cause an allergic-type skin reaction.

• Signs of a fly or mosquito bite may be a raised lump, up to 1cm ($\frac{1}{2}$in) in diameter.

Prevention

• Use flyveils and apply fly repellent ointment applied around the horse's eyes.

• If possible, fit flyscreens on windows and doors of the stable.

• Rug the horse with a fly sheet.

61

Right: Raised lumps on the horse's skin caused by fly or mosquito bites.

• Install pest strips in the stable and use fly spray in the stable and on the horse.
• Frequently remove soiled bedding and manure to a fly-proof manure storage pit.

SNAKE BITE

• Some snakes are poisonous, others are not. The poisonous ones leave two fang marks (puncture wounds), the non-poisonous leave a row of small teeth marks. (The adder is the only poisonous snake in the UK.)
• Because you usually do not see your horse being bitten by a snake, know the signs of snake bite.
• If you do see the snake, take note of its markings to describe it to the veterinarian as there are several different types of antivenene.

Signs

• The horse is stunned, often slobbering from the mouth.
• The horse has staring, unblinking eyes.
• The horse may be wobbly on both fore and hindlegs.
• The horse may be lying on its side or chest.

Action

• Seek veterinary help immediately.

62

If the horse has been bitten on a leg
• Apply a broad bandage with firm pressure over the fang marks and about 7.5cm (3in) either side.
• Calm the horse.

If the horse has been bitten in an area that is difficult to bandage
• Apply an icepack (for example, ice in a towel) to the site to constrict the blood vessels.
• Calm the horse and keep the horse as still as possible to slow the spread of the poison.

Action

Caution
• *Do not* apply a tourniquet as it may aggravate the problem.
• *Do not* cut the skin at the bite site as this will increase the blood flow and spread of the poison.

A horse, while grazing or lying down to rest, may be bitten or stung by an insect, such as a bee, by a spider or come into contact with some plant to which it is allergic. (There are no poisonous spiders in the UK).

UNIDENTIFIED BITE OR STING

Signs will vary but may include:
• Sudden pain and twitching of the skin.
• Rapid swelling or welts on face or body, perhaps with inflammation.
• The horse rubbing or biting the affected area.

Signs

• Look for the cause where the incident occurred.
• If a bee, remove the sting and apply a cold compress or soothing lotion, such as calamine.
• If a spider, identify it and if poisonous, call your veterinarian.
• If the swelling is extensive, or the horse appears distressed or in a state of shock (see page 84), seek veterinary advice.

Action

Bleeder (Epistaxis)

- This term is not to be confused with haemophilia.
- Bleeding is a condition common to racehorses and can be fatal.

Signs

- Bleeding from one or both nostrils after a race, track work or sometimes, swimming.
- Blood may lie inside the nostrils, drip to the ground, or flow freely.
- Some horses bleed in the lungs, signs of which are laboured breathing, distress and coughing.

Action

- Stop exercising the horse immediately.
- Apply an icepack (or ice in a towel) over the upper nose region.
- Run cold water from the hose over the horse's nose.
- Contact your veterinarian.
- Rest is essential for any capillary rupture to heal.
- Feeding the horse at ground level may strengthen capillary blood vessels.

Bleeding

Action

To control the bleeding
- Remain calm.
- Immobilise the horse with a head stall and lead or if this is unsuccessful use another method of restraint (see page 20).
- Apply pressure directly to the site or apply an icepack (or ice in a towel) if the site is inaccessible.
- Apply a bandage firmly to the site (see page 31).

Caution
- *Do not* dab or wipe site as this promotes bleeding.
- *Do not* clean the site until after the bleeding stops.

If blood is oozing slowly
• Apply a clean gauze pad to the wound and direct pressure on it with your fingers.
• After 10 seconds, remove pressure and gauze pad to evaluate the wound.
• If the bleeding recommences, reapply the gauze pad and finger pressure for a longer time, about 20 seconds.

If blood is flowing freely
• Apply a clean gauze pad to the wound and heavy, direct pressure with your clean fingers or hand for about 30 seconds.
• Wrap firmly but not too tightly a 7.5cm (3in) wide adhesive bandage over the gauze pad.
• Leave the bandage in place for 30 minutes then remove to evaluate the wound.
• If bleeding continues, reapply the bandage.

If blood bright red, spurting with pulsating action
• This is a sign of arterial bleeding.
• With gauze pad in hand, apply heavy pressure to site for about 30 seconds,
• Wrap 7.5cm (3in) adhesive bandage tightly around the gauze pad.
• Leave bandage in place and keep the horse immobilised and warm. Call your veterinarian,
• If blood is oozing or running through the bandage, do not remove, but apply another adhesive bandage more tightly over the top.

If blood is coming from an inaccessible area, such as inside the nose
• Apply cold in the form of an icepack, or ice in a towel, and keep the horse immobilised.

Right: Blood trickles from both nostrils, a sign that this horse is a 'bleeder' (see page 64).

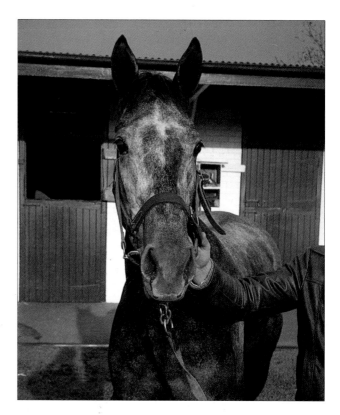

Caution

• Do not panic or hesitate. Stay calm.

• Keep the horse still as movement will accelerate the bleeding. The ideal is for one person to immobilise the horse while another person controls the bleeding.

• When a pressure bandage is left on a limb for 30 minutes, always check the limb below the bandage for swelling, coldness, or no reaction to pain if pinched. If any of these signs is evident, release the bandage and reapply not so firmly.

• Tourniquets are not recommended. They are often difficult to apply and if applied incorrectly, they may accentuate rather than retard bleeding.

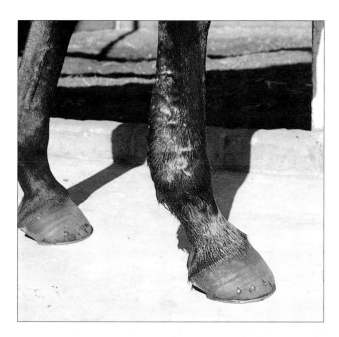

Left: A tendon bows because of the swelling caused by torn or stretched fibrils, inflammatory fluid and capillary haemorrage.

Left: For a chemical burn wash the horse's affected skin thoroughly by hosing for about five minutes.

Bowed Tendon

• The tendons involved in this condition are the superficial and deep flexor tendons.
• The tendons in the front legs are more commonly affected.
• The bow is caused by torn or stretched fibrils, inflammatory fluid, and capillary haemorrhage.

Action

• Contact your veterinarian.
• Apply cold to the swollen tendon by running cold water over the area from a hose for 30 minutes or use an icepack (or ice in a towel) or bandage the swelling with cottonwool (absorbent cotton) soaked in iced water.
• Following the cold treatment, wrap cotton crepe bandage firmly and evenly around the leg from just below the knee to the fetlock joint.
• Rest is important. Tether the horse in the stable.
• If a farrier is available, have the horse shod with a shoe with a raised heel to reduce tension on the tendons.

Burns

• Burns can be caused by chemicals, electricity and heat (boiling water, fires, hot meal plates).
• If more than 50% of the horse's skin is affected, the burn is usually fatal.
• First-degree burns are the least serious; signs are various degrees of reddened skin.
• Second-degree burns are characterised by reddening of the skin with the formation of blisters.
• Third-degree burns are the most serious and are characterised by the full thickness of the skin and underlying tissues being destroyed.

• Extensive second- and third-degree burns are associated with shock, fluid loss (dehydration) and infection.

CHEMICAL BURN Action

• If on skin, wash the skin thoroughly by hosing or pouring copious amounts of water on the area for about five minutes, then gently wash the area with soap and water. Rinse thoroughly.
• If ingested, encourage the horse to drink copious amounts of water. If the horse refuses, use gently running water from the hose to rinse the horse's mouth, thereby stimulating the horse to drink.
• Call your veterinarian.

ELECTRICAL BURN Action

• Turn the power off at the switch.
• If unable to reach the switch, use a dry wooden or plastic stick to flick the plug out of the socket.
• Check breathing and heartbeat (see page 34).
• Call your veterinarian.

HEAT BURN Action

• Immediately run cold water from a hose on the burn for 10 to 15 minutes or immerse the burnt area in a bucket filled with water and ice.
• Dry the area by dabbing gently. Do not rub as you may break the delicate surface.
• In the case of a second- or third-degree burn, protect the wound by gently covering with a gauze pad or clean handkerchief held in place with a light adhesive bandage. Do not use cottonwool (absorbent cotton) because it will adhere to the surface of the burn.
• Deep or extensive burns require quick veterinary attention.

Choke (Choking)

Signs
- Extending head and neck.
- Salivating; grunting; coughing.
- Food and saliva regurgitating through the nostrils.
- Lump may be felt on the left (near) side of the horse's neck.

Action
- Do not allow the horse to drink. Fluid may be taken into the lungs and cause pneumonia.
- If a lump is felt in the horse's neck, gently and firmly massage it up or down, according to its position.

Prevention
- For greedy horses that bolt their feed, place a few large stones in the feed tin.
- Put hay in a hay net.
- Check the horse's teeth every six months for abnormalities.
- Change a horse to boiled grains if it is prone to choke (choking) on dry grains.

Colic

- Those diseases of the horse that cause abdominal pain are generally referred to as equine colic.
- There are numerous types of colic, ranging from mild to severe pain, quick recovery or death.
- There are numerous causes of colic, ranging from teeth abnormalities to excessive low grade roughage, debility, exhaustion, excitement, lush green feed, engorgement with grain and intestinal parasites.

Signs
Depending on the type of colic the signs can vary from being mild to severe.
- Horse dull and restless, pawing the ground and showing spasmodic or continuous pain.

70

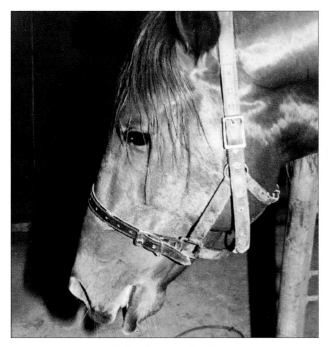

Left: Horse with extended head and neck — a sign of choke.

• Horse continually looking at flank.
• Frequent attempts to urinate; sometimes passes small amounts of dung and gas.
• Abdomen enlarges; horse sweats and is dehydrated.

Action

• Call your veterinarian immediately.
• For some cases, such as impaction colic (constipation), carefully administer orally 5 litres (8½ pints/160fl oz) of paraffin oil.
• If the horse is rolling or thrashing about, fit a head stall and lead and walk the horse. The exercise eases the pain and prevents the horse lying down, rolling and damaging itself.
• Be careful handling horses with colic as sometimes they may react violently.
• Rug the horse if the horse feels cold (on the legs and ears).

Constipation (Foal)

• Severely constipated foals can go into a state of shock and die.
• Constipation occurs more frequently in colts than in fillies.
• The most obvious signs are apparent 12 to 18 hours after the birth.

Signs

• Straining with restlessness; tail cocked.
• Suckling reduced; foal gets up and down; lies flat out or rolls on its back.
• Foal thrashes violently; shock.

Action

If the foal does not pass meconium (thick, dark, tar-like faeces) within 12 hours after birth, give the foal an enema.
• Take care not to damage the lining of foal's rectum and anus.
• Use a disposable, human enema or about 300ml (10fl oz) of warm, soapy water or paraffin oil.

Dehydration

• Horses sweat freely and are more susceptible to dehydration than most animals.
• A horse dehydrates through loss of more fluids and electrolytes from the body than can be replenished by the normal diet.

Signs

• Dry harsh coat; sunken eyes; lethargy.
• Hard dry balls of manure; fatigue, cramping.

Action

• Administer a balanced electrolyte mixture orally by means of feed or drinking water (see page 40).
• Consult your veterinarian, who can administer the electrolytes by a nasal stomach tube or sterile electrolyte solutions by injection.

• *Do not* administer the electrolyte mixture by stomach tube unless you are trained in this procedure. In inexperienced hands the stomach tube may be inadvertently passed into the lungs, resulting in the death of the horse.

Diarrhea

Treating a horse for diarrhea

Signs

• Horse defecates more frequently; faeces are of a porridge-like consistency, often giving off an offensive odour.
• Faeces colour may vary from pale yellow to black with traces of blood and mucous.
• Tail and hindquarters may be matted and discoloured with faeces.
• Horse shows signs of discomfort.
• Horse switches its tail and continually looks at its flank.
• Horse may be off its food; loses weight and shows signs of dehydration and weakness.

Action

• Isolate the horse.
• Reduce the volume of feed by half or give no food at all.
• Remove from the horse's diet succulent lucerne, bran and powdered milk and replace with oaten hay.
• Give the horse frequent small amounts of water with electrolytes (see page 40).
• Check the horse's teeth.
• Reduce the horse's exercise.
• Call your veterinarian if the diarrhea persists for more than 24 hours, there is blood in the faeces, the horse is lethargic, or there is a loss of appetite.

Treating a foal for diarrhea
If diarrhea goes unchecked the foal may die, particularly in the first two days of life.

Signs
- Motion fluid and putrid.
- Foal is lethargic; lacks appetite, may have colic.
- Tail and hindquarters matted and discoloured with faeces.
- Foal is dehydrated, sweating; in shock.

Action
- Call your veterinarian.
- Keep the foal warm and protected from the elements.
- Provide clean water and electrolytes (see page 40).
- Isolate the foal from other foals.
- Restrict the foal's milk intake by milking the mare.
- Frequently remove the mare's dung from the stable.
- Disinfect the stable or box in which foal is housed.

Eye Injuries

- Any injury to the eyeball or eyelids should be regarded as serious.
- Damage to the eyeball may lead to permanent blindness.
- Any break in an eyelid may lead to tear loss and a dry eye.

Action
- Place a wad of cottonwool (absorbent cotton) soaked in water over the eye to keep the eyelid(s) and/or eyeball moist.
- Seek veterinary attention immediately.

FOREIGN BODY IN THE EYE

Foreign bodies such as a grass seed can cause permanent damage to the eye.

Left: Any injury to the eye should be treated as serious.

Left: Gently open and close the eyelid to work the foreign body towards the corner of the eye.

Action
- Wash the eye with copious amounts of water.
- Gently open and close the eyelids to work the foreign body towards the corner of the eyelids or to make it visible.
- If visible, carefully attempt to remove the foreign body.
- If unable to remove, or if after removal the horse is very uncomfortable, seek veterinary assistance.
- Seek veterinary assistance if the horse's eye is tightly closed and you cannot identify the problem.

Foreign Body in the Ear

Signs
- Shaking the head vigorously
- Frequently holding the head to one side
- Rubbing the affected ear.

Action
- Check the ear on the inside and outside.
- Get an assistant to hold the horse's head still.
- Use a torch (flashlight) to examine the ear canal and if discharge is present, clean it out with a cotton bud (swab). If a foreign body is present, it usually comes away with the discharge.
- If the foreign body remains embedded, remove it with blunt-ended tweezers (forceps).
- If you are unable to locate or remove a foreign body and the horse is distressed, call your veterinarian.

Fracture

- The majority of fractures in horses involve limbs.
- In giving First Aid your aim is to prevent the fracture and surrounding injured area from becoming worse.
- If the injured horse is in a danger zone, for example a busy street, move the horse to a safe area for treatment.

• Swelling.
• Pain.
• Holding a leg off the ground.
• Leg(s) misshapen or dangling.

Types of fracture
Clean break A simple, clean-cut break.
Greenstick Only one side of the bone is broken.
Hairline A crack, which may not be through the full thickness of the bone.
Impacted One fractured end of the bone forced into the other.
Multiple The bone is broken in two or more places.
Compound The fractured end of the bone protrudes through the skin. This is a serious fracture because of the danger of infection.

• If the horse has an obvious fracture of the lower limb, apply a splint (see page 38) or a Robert Jones bandage (see page 36) at the site of the fracture to prevent any further damage. Contact your veterinarian immediately.
• In the case of a compound fracture, cover the wound with a gauze wad or clean linen cloth before applying a splint or a Robert Jones bandage.

Frostbite

• Horses exposed to temperatures below freezing point for lengthy periods are susceptible to frostbite.
• The extremities, such as ears and scrotum, are the sites most often affected because of their poorer blood supply and greater exposure.

• The skin is pale, very cold to the touch and has lost sensation.

Right: Holding a limb
from the ground is a
sign of fracture.

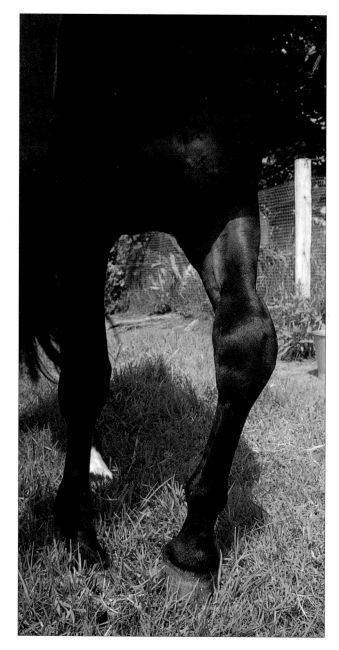

- If wet, dry the horse thoroughly.
- Rug the horse with a heavy-duty wool-lined blanket.
- Warm the frostbitten area by applying a pad soaked in warm water for about 20 minutes.
- If the circulation returns, the skin will become red, swollen and look like a burn.
- If the circulation does not return, and depending on the depth of the frostbite, the skin will peel or a demarcation line will develop between the viable and dead tissue.
- If the superficial skin layers only are peeling, apply a soothing antibiotic cream to soften the skin and control infection.
- If the tissues are pale, cold and insensitive after warming for 20 minutes, call your veterinarian.

Action

Haematoma

Haematoma is a circumscribed swelling of variable size and position, located under the skin and containing blood (see page 82).

- In the early formation of a haematoma, icepacks (or ice in a towel) and cold hosing help to stop bleeding and to reduce swelling.
- If a blood-filled cavity has formed, continue applying icepacks and cold hosing. Call your veterinarian who will drain the haematoma.

Action

Heatstroke

Prolonged heatstroke can lead to coma, brain damage or death.

- Rapid respiration, dilated nostrils.
- Mucus membranes brick red in colour.

Signs

79

- Horse is distressed.
- Uncontrolled and agitated movement.
- Collapse, convulsions, and in some cases, death.

Action

Cool the horse immediately by:
- Removing saddle or rug.
- Cold hosing until temperature returns to normal.
- Providing good ventilation and shade.
- Applying icepacks (or ice in a towel) to the horse's head.
- Providing cool water to drink on the basis of little and often.
- Call your veterinarian.

Hypothermia (Low Body Temperature)

- Hypothermia is most often observed in newborn foals because they are unable to regulate their body temperature.
- A healthy foal subjected to cold conditions normally does not suffer from hypothermia.

Signs

- Initially the foal is restless and cold to the touch.
- Later the foal becomes weak and is uncoordinated. Sucking is weak or stops entirely.
- The foal's temperature is 35°C (95°F) or less.

Action

- Slow, gentle heating can lead to full recovery within 24 hours.
- Keep the foal in the stable and cover with a rug.
- Use heat pads and/or hot water bottles to aid recovery.

Caution
- *Do not* warm the foal rapidly as this can lead to shock and death.

Isoimmune Haemolytic Jaundice

This condition can be compared to Rh disease in human babies and it occurs in newborn foals.

Prevention

• Test the mare's blood before the foal is born. If the result is positive, do not allow milk from that mare to be given to the foal for the first 48 hours.
• Give the foal colostrum from a foster mother or from a supply held in deep freeze for such an emergency.
• Send the mare to a different compatible stallion for the next service.

Signs

• Foal is weak and no longer suckles.
• Breathing is shallow and rapid.
• Foal is anaemic; pale gums and conjunctiva which change to varying shades of yellow.
• After 24 hours urine is dark brown in colour.
• Foal may collapse.

Action

• Call the veterinarian immediately.
• If the foal is less than 48 hours old, prevent the foal from suckling the mare by muzzling the foal or removing the mare.
• Give the foal colostrum from another source. Colostrum is only produced by the mare for about the first 24 hours after the foal is born and the foal can only absorb the antibodies from it for about the first 36 hours of life.
• The mare should be milked out hourly and the milk discarded.
• After 48 hours, allow the foal to return to the mare to suckle naturally.

Right: Haematoma on the chest. (See page 79).

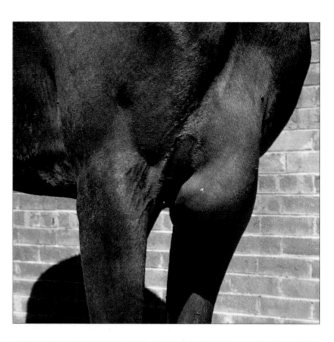

Right: Drainage of a haematoma.

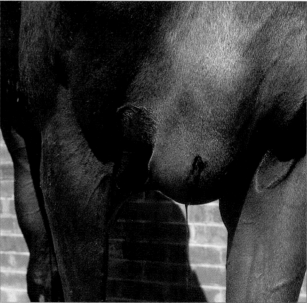

Nail Prick

The horse is said to be "pricked" if, when shoeing, a nail is placed incorrectly on the inside of the white line or, when being driven, the nail crosses the white line and penetrates sensitive tissues of the foot.

Signs

- Mild lameness shortly after shoeing.
- Horse may be lame 3 to 7 days after shoeing.
- Hoof wall warm to touch.
- Often pastern is swollen.
- Horse exhibits signs of pain when pressure is applied over offending nail.

Action

- Leave the shoe off.
- Remove any debris and dirt.
- Using a clean hoof knife, enlarge the hole to allow for proper drainage.
- Clean around the nail hole with tincture of iodine (anti-bacterial, anti-fungal solution).
- Soak the hoof in hot water for 10 minutes three times a day. Take care the level of water does not cover the coronary band of the hoof.
- Fill the hole with drawing agent, such as magnoplasm, or paint the hole with tincture of iodine.
- Cover the sole with an adhesive bandage to prevent further contamination.
- Call your veterinarian to administer antibiotics and tetanus antitoxin.

Poisoning

- Poisoning is not common in horses.
- Accidental contamination of feed, pastures or water or an accidental overdose when drenched for internal parasites are the most common causes of poisoning in horses.

Prevention

• To avoid poisoning, make sure all toxic substances are kept out of the horse's reach.
• In laying baits for vermin or spraying pasture with herbicides and pesticides, make sure the horse has no access to the areas while the products are toxic.

Signs

Individually or collectively, the following signs do not conclusively indicate poisoning:

• Depression; loss of appetite and weight loss.
• Laboured breathing
• Dehydration, salivation, diarrhea
• Twitching muscles; wobbling, convulsions
• Paralysis, coma.

Action

• Contact your veterinarian immediately.
• If poisoning is due to something ingested, give the horse 5 litres (8½ pints/160fl oz) of mineral oil by mouth. Do not give mineral oil if there are signs of diarrhea (see page 73).
• If the horse is hyper-excitable, wobbly or paralysed, provide plenty of straw bedding to prevent injury.
• Place the horse in a dark, quiet stable.
• Supply drinking water containing electrolytes to prevent dehydration.
• If shock is setting in (see below), warm the horse.
• If snake bite, see page 62.
• Keep the horse as quiet as possible. Movement will stimulate circulation of the poison.

Shock

• Shock is a term used to describe a state of collapse.
• Shock may range from mild to severe, and can bring about total collapse, coma and death.
• Shock usually results from some physical trauma, often in accident cases and is often associated with blood loss, poison, infection or dehydration.

- Weakness, lying down.
- Rapid, weak pulse.
- Pale gums and conjunctiva.
- Rapid, shallow breathing.
- Horse is cold to the touch.

Signs

- Calm the horse.
- Keep the horse warm with a rug to maintain normal body temperature.
- Control any bleeding (see page 34).
- In cases other than mild shock, call your veterinarian for immediate treatment.

Action

Wounds

- Most wounds in horses are contaminated.
- Antibiotic and tetanus antitoxin injections by your veterinarian should be considered.
- Wounds are classified as abrasions, contusions, incised wounds, lacerations and puncture wounds.

- The normal abrasion is painful to the touch, haemorrhages a little and more often than not is contaminated with debris.
- Caused by friction between the horse's body and a hard surface, such as a roadway. The hair and surface layer of skin, and sometimes the underlying tissues, are removed.

**ABRASIONS
Signs**

- Clean the wound by spraying or by running water from a hose onto it. Water pressure should be sufficient to wash out debris but not so strong as to drive the debris into the damaged tissue. Alternatively, clean the wound initially with 3% hydrogen peroxide.
- When the wound is clean, pat it dry with clean gauze, then dust or spray it with an antibiotic.

Action

85

Right: A deep abrasion should be thoroughly cleaned of all debris before treatment.

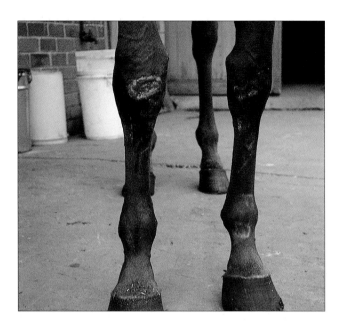

• Leave the abrasion open to the air to dry but if oozing freely, cover with a gauze pad and bandage, and finally with an adhesive bandage until the oozing stops (see page 31).

Caution
• *Do not* exercise the horse until healing is obvious if the abrasion is large.
• If the abrasion is deep, exposing bone, tendons and so on, contact your veterinarian immediately.

CONTUSIONS
Signs

•Contusions are characterised by bruising and swelling of the skin and underlying tissues. They are not necessarily associated with a break in the skin.
• Caused by a kick, fall or collision.

Action

• If there is a break in the skin, call your veterinarian who will administer antibiotics and tetanus antitoxin.

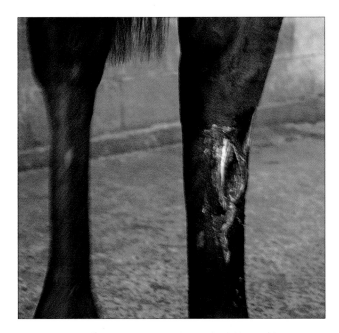

Left: A deep laceration to the leg.

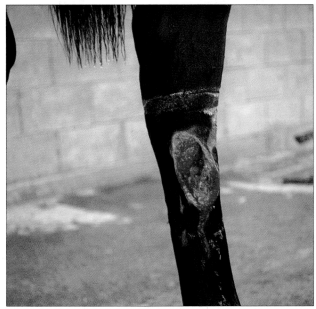

Left: Continue to keep the laceration bandaged until fleshy tissue fills the cavity to skin level.

• If there is no break in the skin, the swelling is best dealt with by the application of alternate hot and cold compresses.

Hot compress

— Put hot water into a bucket containing 2 tablespoons of salt. The temperature of the water should be so hot that you can *just* put your hand into the water and leave it there.

— Drop a large wad of cottonwool (absorbent cotton) in the hot salt water solution then hold it on the contused area until it cools off.

— Repeat this procedure for five minutes, morning and night, and follow it with cold compresses for the same length of time.

Cold compress

— Hose the swollen area with a fair amount of water pressure. The cold constricts the blood vessels and the pressure has a massaging effect.

INCISED WOUNDS
Signs

• Characteristics of these wounds are clean-cut, fairly well-opposed edges and minimum tissue damage.
• Caused by broken glass or similar sharp object.

Action

• If bleeding, apply pressure directly to the wound with a clean gauze pad or linen cloth until the bleeding stops (see page 34).
• Clean the wound only if necessary.
• Gently but firmly pinch the opposing edges of the wound together.
• Apply thin strips of adhesive bandage in a criss-cross formation about 1cm (½in) apart directly across the wound.
• Place a gauze pad over the wound and secure with a firm adhesive bandage. This will also help to immobilise the edges of the wound (see page 31).
• Confine the horse.

• Leave the bandage in place for 48 hours, then check the wound.
• If the wound is clean, dry and showing no sign of inflammation, rebandage and change the dressing every 48 hours.

Caution
• If the wound is extensive (long and/or deep) contact your veterinarian to have it stitched.
• Such wounds should be stitched within eight hours.
• The stitches will be removed 10 to 12 days later.

LACERATIONS
Signs

• The edges of the wound are often irregular, jagged and gaping. Sometimes whole sections of the skin and underlying tissues are torn away.
• Lacerations are usually not painful and haemorrhage is variable.
• Caused by barbed wire, sharp edge of a tin, and so on.

Action

• Thoroughly clean the wound by hosing or by applying 3% hydrogen peroxide.
• Remove any hair, dead tissue or foreign bodies from the wound.
• Apply antibiotic powder.
• Cover the wound with a gauze pad then a gauze bandage, both held firmly in place by an adhesive bandage (see page 31).
• Call your veterinarian as the laceration may need to be stitched.
• If unable to be stitched, leave the bandage in place for two days.
• When the bandage is removed, hose the wound to clean away any discharge, debris or dead tissue and dress as before.

• Continue the bandaging until fleshy tissue has filled in the cavity to skin level. Then leave the bandage off, allowing the air and sunshine to dry the surface of the wound.
• Restrict exercise until the skin has completely covered the wound.

PUNCTURE WOUNDS

• Puncture wounds are generally painful and may or may not be accompanied by haemorrhage.
• Caused by penetration of the skin or hoof by a splinter, piece of wire, nail, and so on.

Action

• Carefully clip the hair away from the hole.
• Carefully check the wound to see that no foreign body remains embedded.
• Clean the area with 3% hydrogen peroxide and dab the wound with tincture of iodine.
• Keep the wound open as long as possible while drainage is taking place.
• If the puncture appears to penetrate through the skin into the underlying tissues, contact your veterinarian who will administer antibiotics, tetanus antitoxin and provide drainage if necessary.

INDEX

*Page references in **bold type** refer to descriptions of symptoms. Page references in italic type refer to illustrations.*

ACKNOWLEDGMENTS

I would like to thank my wife Jan and children Melanie, Samantha, Damien and Edwina for their patient support during the time of writing.
My sincere thanks to my father Eric for his diligent assistance in planning, researching and proofreading, and also to my sister Judy Shields for undertaking the daunting task of deciphering my notes and transferring them to print.

TIM HAWCROFT